Drifting to "Hello"

Praise for Drifting to "Hello"

"The poems in this welcome collection of Fred Gerhard's work range considerably: from Victorian rooms to the Pennsylvania and New England landscapes he knows intimately; from the psychology of inner experience to the dance of interpersonal relationships; from the noise of the trains that run through all of our lives (and occasionally crash into walls) to the quiet of the "dark grape taste of twilight." Likewise, Gerhard's diverse poetic techniques run the gamut from lucid and conversational free verse to skillful and musical rhyme. Throughout, he crafts memorable lines and indelible images, giving (as he puts it in his tribute to Edgar Allan Poe) "consonant to forlorn sound"—and to the sound of joy."

—Simon Hunt, author of *Lesser Magi* and *Endlings*

"With attention to detail and a willingness to play with form, Gerhard's poems open us to the world, whether it's to "Cascading ice" or "The regular clop and / Clack of rail joints / Shouldering our steel / Wheels." These poems tap gently at our door and invite us to join the dance of dandelions and red catkins, bobcats and trolleys, of life and death and love."

—Barbara Morrison, author of *Terrarium, Here at Least,* and *Innocent.*

"In Fred's poetry, there is a magical sense of loss, and light—an odd combo, indeed, but there nonetheless—that envelops the reader in something mystical. I am ever-grateful that he, in many ways, opened the world of poetry to me. I hope you enjoy walking his halls as much as I do."

—Kirk Lawrence-Howard, *BespokeVocals.com*

"The poems in this collection are warm and inviting. The journey from *Pinewoods* to *Returning Home* leaves the reader warm-hearted. You don't want to simply drift to them; you want to immerse yourself in every word on every page. With a gentle hand, the poems leave the reader feeling thoughtful and spirited—an enchanting read."

—Melissa Dorval, author of the novel *When You Lose Control*

"One can easily discover bliss in the imaginative and playful ways Gerhard uses language. But behind his words is the steady pulse of a heart that feels every moment of joy in life, from the magic of the mundane dandelion to the ways of seeing God. We are the lucky ones who get to experience his many loves through his poems."

—Kevin Scott Hall, songwriter and author of *A Quarter Inch From My Heart* and *Off the Charts!*

DRIFTING TO "HELLO"

Poems by
Fred Gerhard

Khotso Publishing
Peterborough, NH

Drifting to "Hello"
Copyright © 2023 by Fred Gerhard. All rights reserved. No part of this book may be used or reproduced in any manner whatsoever without written permission except in the case of brief quotations embodied in critical articles or reviews. For information, contact the publisher at 87 Wilder Farm Road, Peterborough, NH 03258.

Gerhard, Fred
Drifting to "Hello"
Khotso Publishing, 2023
ISBN 978-1-7375868-5-2

Cover painting, *Cape Code Sunset*, by Sophia Januszewski.

for Rachael

x

Contents

Dancing Through Pinewoods

Dance 3
The Mushroom Garden 4
On the Surface 5
New England Dulcimer 6
All You Need Bring 7
Walk With Me 8
Darkening Trees 9
This Time Around 10
Teine Sith 11
Help! I Need Some Body 13
Untitled 14
The String 15
Slow Silver 16
Falling Song 17
Open Sway 18

A Day in June

Seeing 21
A Day in June 22
Not Me 23
My Heart Ensnared 24
i and you 25
Emptying Clouds 26
Dandelion Fairy 27
Shadow Fences 29

Autumns

New Season 33
On the Steps 34
Autumn Will 35
Kerouac Rain 36
Fatigues 37
Need Not 38
Disassembled 39
Waiting to Rain 40
Atmosphere 41
Arroyo 42
The Paper Door 43
Against Gray 44
Stasis 45
Going On 46

Revelations

Chill November 49
Corner Seat in an Ashburnham Gallery 50
The Cart Path 51
The Way 53
In Reply 55
New Vision 56
Maple Wings 58
Gray Hullaballoo 59
A Kinder Solitude 60
Crossing the Dark Wing 61
Closest Thing 62
Ajar 64
Attic Haunt 65
Presence 66
Uncoiling 67
Voice Above the Waves 69

Returning Home

- The Sea, The Sea 73
- First Drop 74
- Telescope 76
- Sunward 77
- Sundown 79
- Blacklight 80
- Rogue 81
- Eclipse 82
- If I Say I am Afraid 84
- 189 85
- Trolley Museum 87
- A Train Runs Through 89
- Orbisonia Dawn 90
- Altered State 92
- Daring Duo 94
- Prodigal 96
- I Was a Psychologist 97
- What to do with the Body— 99
- Seed 101
- What To Do 102
- Returning Home by Pleasant Street 103

Notes 106

Acknowledgments 109

Gratitude 112

About the Author 115

Dancing Through Pinewoods

Dance

To dance
        To learn
                Lifted up into

The circle
        By the hands that

First lifted you up
        Into life

Family became
        Dance

And Dance extended to
        All the world
                Willing

A smile
        A hand

A good will to turn
        Together

The Mushroom Garden

Periwinkle constellations unwind
hardly visible pushing up through heavy pine
needles deep in the scent of the Great Pine's lore
songs before before
push up, push up
hard

as teeth
from the forest floor

On The Surface

The picnic friend who rides with you
Asks on a nameless pond
Of anonymous water
Who you are.

The spring, the rain, and the dew
Which her fingers pursue
Become your memories
In a conversation of rippled sense

Drifting to
"Hello."

Farewell comes as soon
In the heavy lagoon
At the shore
Where the depth is the surface,

Glass tears from an oar
Discarded, you hear
As they reflect
Not on the water.

New England Dulcimer

In safely wooded
New England dawn
Sings the heart of an
Empty dulcimer —

> *Cast no shadow,*
> *Voice no sound,*
> *Time's most shallow*
> *Turn's profound.*

When every string
Has said its song
The sun will pass
To watch you dawn.

All You Need Bring

Bring drink from the water
To let my heart flow
Down through the branches
Of getting old.

Bring spice for the tea
To color life's dreams.
Wait while you can.
It's only steam.

Bring smoke for the candle
To hang up a flame,
Lighter than a postmark
Rides a name.

Bring songs for the dance
Circles made of hands,
Wheels for the flight
In case we land.

Bring you for a stay.
It's all you need bring.
I've me for a place,
And too many things.

Walk With Me

Walk with me
I am still walking
With you

Our feet leave no mark
The forest floor
Keeps falling

Branches, twigs
Pine needles
Bodies and ribbons

Seasons and songs
You spoke
As we searched

A path out of the
Deeper wood beyond
The breath on our lips

That earthy scent
Long after the tune
Turned dark

Darkening Trees

The darkening trees do not argue
with the light or the autumn pall
but wait wide-leafed
for colors of fall

Before we fall in cold slumber
let me not argue your fading
but wait open-bodied, open-palmed
darker waters wading

This Time Around

Imagine the uprooted stump of your life
cut clear of foliate fancies
all the bared tendrils pungent rife
with your dark wet soul
ripped and broken from filament memory
                     torn

a unique individual disconnected
the tangle of your days exposed
recalling child hands
child arms descending
silvery as meadow moonlight recognized
                     as your own

holy ghost arriving to cup to hold to bestow
the coppery dust of your life
the very metal of you
become light
to turn a leaf tarnished
                     and tawny

this time around
start at the heartwood exposed
the expanse of rings
encircling
all that went
                     before

Teine Sith

Give me arrows of reed
Give me throat of wren
Loose me in a meadow of papyri
Birch-bark forests glowing white and pungent
    Dip my finger in your darkness
    And draw in secret letters
Derived from a primrose pact
Turn my head with a glance
    A demure look of nonchalance
    And abandon me to my reverie
In inebriated tiredness
I scribble hypnogogic visions
    Across the remainder of a note
    I do not send

Give me the full stanza
The knell of the rhyme
    Returning the slap in the
    Bell cast of my torso a
Deafening song of life
My pen will roll in fingers
    Like Hitodama deciding
    Which way to alight
And carry a message to you
Where you dare read
    A madness for life
    A madness for joy or pain
Or both

And the poem is unlike a
Page of inked words
    As unlike as a landscape
    from the iridescent paint of
A shimmering vista
Glimmering
    Glowing and
    Gone

Help! I Need Some Body

We emptied our bodies
at the first glance —
    glowing souls spirited
    dance to the ginger taste
    of tongues, touching, suspending
    the need to breathe

Chest-fall, crest fallen
left alone
    the rolled-out stone
    a mossy heart gathering
    no pity or sleep
    or death

But to lie here where you
swept pine needles clear for us
    and after offered
    a pale hand
    to draw me
    to my feet

In the moment
of helping the moment move on
    all was
        lost

Untitled

Before the ice is in the pools —
— Emily Dickinson, "37"

Cascading ice is melting now
That granite's clothed in sun —
Drips and licks a salty hollow
For its glimmering run

Far from this snow-clad solstice day
We danced clothed in sweat —
Wove and dove a summer less grave
Where breath less current met —

How cold you've turned the flow of life
Where rivulets combine —
Pulsing from the one you call ice —
To the one you call mine —

The String

I'm the string
Who sang under the spell
Of her bow
And lingered after the song was done.

I'm the string
Who wept beneath the touch
Of her fingers
And whispered the memory after the song.

I am the string
Upon the neck,
Lace upon the nape,
Safe in velvet,
Going out of tune.

Slow Silver

Afternoon sky silver behind cloud
mountains shining like a ghostly tune

The final petite daisies of summer
blaze across forest floor in farewell
when daisies are no more

If you should stand near to see
this sylvan glade —
and touch my sleeve

For a moment the forest observes

Not even the leaves breathe
a word

Falling Song

There's a penny whistle
On the water
Singing like the daughter
Of autumn.

The breath under her fingers
Rends your heart to linger,
But you may never find her
For her song.

She'll play the mist to rise,
From shore to shore reprise,

And all in falling
For autumn.

Open Sway

Open at the hard bottom
of what we weave from
hooping looping birdsong

Open we
let in
light, water, breeze

Open pine trees
gifting ginger blonde quills spilled
to cup and keep
forever

Open to thrown days
fixed by fire
and wire and glaze

Open domiciles
for hummingbird hearts
exposed

Open the pinewood glade
of love
visible one to another

Opened lovers
cull a space
awaiting return

that hangs open in you
forever swaying
for more

A Day in June

Seeing

I see twice — the double-take.
And your surprise in the next moment
When I glimpse your smile.

It is like this with everything
We say after words —
Even what we miss in seeing

    And need not see.

A Day in June

You are like a day in June
That I might feel your warmth,
A day in spring, blossoming,
That I might smile in turn,
Your eyes, your intelligence, and how
I might meet your gaze
Long as the days in June
Drawing out some gentle new life
Among the wildlife opening us,
Washed in sun and water,
In shades of green breezes.
You are a day in June,
And I, but a man in the daylight,
Warmer for being near
One who throws my shadow so clearly.

Not Me

I open my mouth
And someone I don't know walks out
And kisses you
And cries for you
And readily dies for you
For he never has to be
And again it is not me

My Heart Ensnared

What will be,
Oh Muse, for me?
What garden have you prepared?

What sweet flower
In greening showers
Will drench my heart ensnared?

I know you well
And I can tell
The one who plots surprise.

The muse awaits
Just at my gate
To draw my heart aside,

And beating fast
My love is cast
For the muse has caught my eye.

My heart is tossed
Helpless, lost
In hopes of loving blind.

i and you

    separated by

                          and

    alone

    i
    you
    have no shadow

                        i and you

    do not cast

                          and

                         and

    holds
    until eternity

    do
    we
    meet

                        i and you

    orbit
    belief

Emptying Clouds

Stand me in this rain
Until I am drenched
Let the pain fall
In its strange drizzle
Every light slight
Condensing on my brow
Each loss invisible
Misting
My shadow
On the back of my neck
I know your pitiless kiss
Down matted arms
Dark veined hands
Rivulet fingers
Streaming away
All I was
Lost in the wildly turning storm
And all we were —

Emptying clouds
Looking for some sign
Of daybreak blue
And memory of warm

Dandelion Fairy

The English Garden returned this spring,
tulips tall and strong
opening first, hovering in
May breeze waiting for phlox and
fuchsia to join the Victorian
afternoon garden party on the lawn.

And gazing long from the lawn
to see pink, white, magenta petals,
I absently drew my finger across your
lips, collecting yellow pollen —
a dandelion fairy in the grass, here today
in full yellow blaze of sun,
sitting at ease in the verdant afternoon,
and free upon the gentle green
rippling day.

I would not pick you from your
fuzz-lined stalk or your tale
about living for a day,
but listening to your golden plea, Alaya,
I touched your yellow face, amber heart,
powdery joy knowing
you cannot be planted, or tamed
for English Gardens or painted ladies.

And in a madness I have fallen in love
with a dandelion sprite, even knowing that
the will of the wisps of us
tomorrow blows away to nothing,
scattering our hopes to the wind,
dancing pa de deux currents to alight
only upon a planet too small
to contain
        our garden in bloom.

Shadow Fences

The shadow of her eyelash
Falls upon her cheek
Lighter than your touch.

A sword of innocence
It falls upon your heart,
And you shadow it with touch.

Autumns

New Season

Sounds of brown leaves
Scraping the windy curbs
And the clinks of bicycle chains
Changing gears
The smell of a new season
In the clear air.
It's the heartbeat of a day
With nothing to do.

On the Steps

Everyone's got tomorrow
Hanging up their sleeve
Well out of sight.
Sitting on the steps
To stone-blue weather's bite,
Planning to wait
For plans to
Come true.

And I have seen myself
Strapped in rush-machines
Flying for the sun
And not the sight.
Balance to the hearts
Who tear into sleep
Where no one wakes
With tears,
And some we'll
Not forget.

Autumn Will

autumn will come
I will be broken
hearted
it will be
all right

all right
being broken
hearted
I will it

but anyway
autumn comes

Kerouac Rain

This is Kerouac rain
Hits the road
Like it knows
What's coming
Asphalt humming
          Drumming
          Mumbling
    Rain was
    Wet is
    All is watery
    All is wet
Drive on rain
Drive on
Drive on
      Road rage rain really
Open blank-faced water balls
        Meditating on the black-top to nowhere

Fatigues

Some burn out. Some burn on.
Some of them just get burned.
Etched in chalk, bored of talk
Of wearing guns and ferns.

Some see light in the forest.
Others just see trees.
I close my eyes to these and see
Friendship's lovely breeze,

And I hold on.

Need Not

I need not fly
I fold my wings
I bow my head
I wait for things

I need not feel you
Everywhere
I need not breathe
In so much air

I need not listen
When you don't call
I need no wisdom
I need not fall

I need not want
To know you well
I need not need
You at all

Disassembled

to be myself　　　　means
　　　to be　　　　my story
private moments　　recalled,
ordered into　　　　words
oracle vowels　　　inaudible
　　　shared here in a letter
　　　　　to you

who may not reply
in the safety of
your　　　　　　　self
kept　　　a　　　　　　part
　　　still my story remains
my　　　　　　self
　　　dis　　as　　sem　　bled

I hand you the pieces
　　　　　one by one
　　　　　　　　like sand

Waiting to Rain

It's waiting to rain.
Moths too damp to fly
Have gone insane on my screen.
They cry moth tears.

Down the hill the water
Laughs too loudly.
I cannot separate the waves
From the water
And I drown in my frustration.

      A poet tells me
      "It's so sad."
      But he's never been here.

It's waiting to rain
As I battle overcoats
For princesses I don't love,
And my honesty makes me
Less the hero,

And before it can rain,
Water rushes over my hill
From below
And merrily suffocates me.

It's waiting to rain,
But it's not waiting for me.

Atmosphere

The descending tone of a single prop
rises to a steady hum lost in atmosphere
I breathe — and again —
quieter, listen

three notes of a truck in reverse
three blocks away
warning transmitted even to me
the intention to go back
through blind spots

the first sounds of an SOS
injury is possible, listening for
what lifts off from the ground
or rolls back heavy as time
under the wheel

there's much more I do not hear:

    my breath repeating,
    squirrel talons down walnut bark,
    oak leaf scuffling over fallen copper
comrades
    to no avail, catching
    the momentary lift
    that slid the glinting plane out of view
    carried the warning thrice intoned,

    glancing to the courtyard

    I forgot to mention
    the breath I held
        listening for you.

Arroyo

Catkins are red on last year's dead, dried, leaves
where we walked their crimson carpeted path
only a season before the year cleaved
vermillion streams to where a river swath
ran full and wild, and sang in each of us,
and down the red trails I wander for you,
knowing you must follow a scarlet loss
with fluttering calls like a cardinal who
is listening to a silent sunset,
where embers spread and deepen to twilight.
I find you no longer here in the red
flow of some salty arroyo gone dry,
but wander the bed of an old cracked road
you've left me for a path I cannot know.

The Paper Door

cloth and paper masks hide the living
reveal the dead
      their mouths

dark wasp withstands a cold day in sunlight
after building a paper house
      to outlast life

these paper poems, too, reveal or mask
do not realize death,
      folded, propped

like me standing at an open door
in an October emptying of notions
      and warmth

letting go the safety of paper
I sit by the wasp
      on gray boards

in the waning light on the porch
until we are cold and beyond parting
      or paper

Against Gray

Now only of wind,
Of wood,
And tattered banners
Huddling together.
      One last stand,
One final rebellion,
Bright and dimming
Alone against the gray.

Stasis

in the cream clear as ice
wired in stasis
moments of colorful mouths
uncurl rows of fern-like teeth

opening in the deep blue
gloss of memory
water is moving
speaking in tongues

look closely
it's you,   you,   you
you see

through the reflection, what unfurls
flowers   ferns   ice
grown still on the other side
behind what froze
is
you

melting, loosing
trapped atmosphere
bobbling from fall
into spring

breathe it in
flowing cold as winter
burbling
beneath the year

Going On

Reality is snow in your collar
Stinging of something you know
but forgot was going on.

I'm going on. Are you?
On the other side of snow,
beyond the prickling sky,
across the road.

Or like so many friends quiet
as snow, have you fallen
for the cold?

Here then
is my small warmth —
Just as real.

Revelations

Chill November

On a chill November afternoon
memory of color
clings to sky
like pitch dark twigs alive
reaching for a summer sun
long gone

a poorly dreamt expanse
of slate fog
pearly mist
far away and departing
our lives
our graves

leaves space for
autumn hymns in the
low quiet tone
that falling breezes
know
and hum

where we would go
before we let go
and throw
our shivering limbs alive
to the ghostly maw
of the year

Corner Seat in an Ashburnham Gallery

An old plank worn smooth
In a corner by a window
In a black and white photo

Hung in the corner by the window
Of the gallery in Ashburnham

A creative connection
A convergence of sorts

Perhaps someone will
Pray here

The Cart Path

Stepping from pavement
a cart path appears, lost to time,
overgrown, green gullies.
I step into weeds,
sapling trees, wheel-rut stream
trickling, twinkling to me.

What startles from undergrowth
flapping for boughs and sky —
a fluttering of wings and things
flashing in me.

A breath. Focus. Quiet.
The question only feet
can answer.
Disappearing deeper
I don't leave a trace.

Forest reclaims,
folding back behind
careful calves,
my legacy stepping away
toward the unknown where
none travel,
but did.

I listen for them long.
I call at the gate gone,
the cellar holes, coke ovens,
mossy mill stone.

Let the ghosts of cattle rise hazy,
graze again field filled
with greening
granite boulders.

All that growing and going
by a path I ran deftly past for years —
A breeze.
And why?

Again the flutter for flight.
Caged ribs tighten
by a taut-barked birch,
a torso reaching —
aiming for light and night —
a destination unseen.

Down every trail lost in growth
there is one moment in the waning light —
boots stayed.
Standing.

Do I return now?
Now?

And what beckons?

The Way

You'd think I was crazy if I told you
I saw God once.
      So I won't.

But I sought Jesus who was the Way
and made me examine what being
and Way-ing might imply,

and Buddha who showed a Way
only to be deified,

and Tao, ever the Way.

Every night I empty these from my head.

As a small child I dreamt a sky-high figure,
soaring black and white, and it rumbled,
      and I knew.

Working in the Holyoke projects
I saw a small girl with carefully braided hair
riding her daddy's tan shoulders, laughing
      and I saw.

One summer, entering a Quaker silence,
another room opened in me, more silent,
and warm, where a light reached down from
behind and held me like a child in arms of light,
      and I felt.

To say that I saw God once
is a lie.

Here
in me
I cannot unsee God
or the way
of God.

In Reply

Let it be reality.
Let it become.
Let it be what it is.
Don't let it succumb.
Let it be. Don't disturb.
Have nothing to do.
Let it be all divine.
Let it be you.

New Vision

I am not wearing my glasses for this
blind as faith I chisel a tomb
up for revisions and visions unclarified
by eyes and lenses hemming away at me

There are sweet babes in this sovereign world
reign of brimstone men in houses
white as snow-blind light struck dumb
enough to rain hell on the small dells
tenements, tenants, hovels, and tree houses

In the heart of trees run through like Jesus
hands and feet are babes sweet, the only
thing left in split heartwood scent
and I defend them with sword or word
or mightier — tears — amplified lines
from bards gone deep — deeper than my

heart would or could follow —
I fall and lead a less quiet desperation
to protect hope's small cry
born this morning to a masked world
ruled by red-brimmed death
when life is the thing with wings
every small feathered fluttering

babe placed in your palm
uncurls your fingers — look —
look — the birth line, death line crossroads
all the same — your tender palm warm
capable of rounding capes unmapped
topographical hands of good hope
with rivulet veins

open-fisted, open fisted

Rising — we are the same
palm to palm in the allemande
caress whispering to a night
breathing copper-zinc inhalation
through old screen doors
and all that insomnia waiting
for dreams to see — really see
a new vision

Maple Wings

Dew circle droplets dawdle
on the page of a body
on the forest floor —
exposed text illustrating
unnerving patience

in sympathetic systems
which unaware
sprout wings of maple
patiently grown through
the hole in a heart
and shoulder blade —

Wings!
split a cocoon body
syrupy, seeking light
in dappling day —
my sweet maple wings
facing the ground
        I no longer walk

Gray Hullaballoo

Gray sky hullaballoo
like a lid on the afternoon —

Dim with thought
I turn from the window —

dingy-hearted
day bereft of hours —

A heartbeat curled
against chill —

My joy is hibernating —

My God is very still

A Kinder Solitude

After a year of living alone
I have come to know me.
At times I hate what I see
or who I thought was me.
But then a kinder solitude

of me in birdsong bleating,
insistent as the breeze, slow
hollow call of a car on the road,
the words I read sleepily nodding
me or wanting me to repeat them,

or write them into being.
The empty space of this room.
Wooden walls' settling tune: pops, cracks,
to be left alone and consider how
your absence is also me —
no longer waiting.

Crossing the Dark Wing

I know the man who walks
these Victorian floors by night
in the insomnial dark   the other one
the conductor in black   the phantom
      the golem

Sometimes he stares too long
at a window   or a painting
and I catch a glimpse of him
      and he of me   standing
very still   we don't speak

I want only to retreat
perchance   to live
      avoiding his path
I cross the room   quick
      hitting
      hard

granite counter
where I did not know it
could be   in the pitch
night

dislodging   my hip
      we pass

angel knuckles   swell
beneath a dark wing
I fold
      in pain

Closest Thing

Could the night be any more secretive?
I don't know.
I don't know.

Could the day stand being repeated?
In a dream.
In a dream.

Could the ghost of empty hours
howl in the towers
of a night pulled to powers
pallid and torn?

    "I could.

    I could,"
came a voice
of someone speaking
at my ear.

    "I could,"
from lips
out of breath,
very near.

    "I could
make the night more hollow.

   I could make the hallowed
ground slope from
the creek
and run a trickle
cold and dark
right down your soul
from your upturned tongue
to your feet,
embedded where you stand.

   I could
collapse this night
with fear and hope.

   I could.

   I could if I wanted,
dim
the light within.

   I could,"

     said the closest thing
     to me.

Ajar

the door is
worn where paint peels
along the faceplate

the door is
partway open —
ceramic knobs like ears

but the jarring thing
is I don't recall
opening it

or touching the knob

I am
standing witness
to a ghost

staring back
to the door
      ajar

Attic Haunt

for Edgar

What haunts you find in cold attics
Where wind intrudes — a wall admits
A whistling tone you stop to hear —
Your pen poised with poem near.

After a pause, you write it down,
Give consonant to forlorn sound,
The ghostly poet given pen
Gives lines to one alone again.

If you can haunt yourself so well
What solace does a sound dispel
When numbing attic howls impart
A chill –– a kiss –– for ghostly art?

Presence

When you died
    The astonishing thing was
How present you were
    And alive.
You followed me everywhere
    Asking to dance, to go on long walks,
To brew tea,
    To sit out on the porch in the May breeze
    And listen to the bumble bees.
You slid between the blankets for a long nap
And bleary-eyed smiled to see me in the mid-
    Afternoon when you awoke.
How did I become so loved by you
    So late in the game?
And here you are picking out a soft cotton shirt
For me to wear.
    I place my hands deep into the
    Black and gray garden we plant today,
And feel for life
    Deep in the cool dirt
As you comment on the salty smell of the
    Sweat on my neck,
Laughing because you can't get sun burnt,
    And the blood is hot where I
        Was once pale.

Uncoiling

for Steve

We hike this hill together
as the morning streams sol
in the month of solstice.

Ascending souls we rise by rushing thighs
through rippling wheat, wild
and sweet grasses unnamable

To the crest, run, pound the ground
to rise, to arrive
atop the mowed meadow mound,

The tangle in me tangling you,
blood thumping fluid valves through
heated breaths in rising breast.

Wasn't it you who told me,
"In each of us there is a small sea
and a blaze to set free?"

My small heart parts a red sea
cupped in my furnace chest again
catching my breath – catching in –

The thing about talking, or walking
with the dead is you find them
in everything —

Even this mountaintop — you
untangling our lives to two strands

to stand guard over the swath of us,

One, the ocean, aquamarine,
the other, fire burning orange,
and in between I ask you,

"How do I follow?
How do I find you
to weave again water and sun?"

Silence — dripping
the tipping year,
the ocean in me reflecting your flame —

"Both point to the sky.
We fly!" you reply,
And gazing to the rising haze

A cloudless blue continues to move
up and through,
uncoiling me
    to you.

Voice Above the Waves

I have avoided reading
        What they wrote about you
Knowing this time you will die

Who was content to live in spirit
        Come back as ghost
I think we spoke in tongues

Madness of love elated, known deeply
        My heart again, again
As it must repeat for you, for me

I know I will open the word
        Listen to the voice on the water
Pushing off from shore

Were you ever really there?
        Your friends' small boat
Pale wedge on twilight ripples

Smoothed in dark lapping dreams
        Hard to make out
Drifting to the far side

You must be the one
        Asleep — astern
Far from the prow.

Returning Home

The Sea, The Sea

There are mysteries in the seas
    In the depth and weight of
      All that cold saline running
Into and through the flashing splash-point
    You dive for
But landlocked in your little town
      The New England sun beating down
Liquid-bright on the hapless beauty
    Of your English garden

Landlocked in your house
    Where you drift from room to room
      Locked in the land of your skin
Where the salty red pillar of you
    Asks "wherefore all the salt
Why all the waves, wounds making wakes
    Cresting in your chest
Like a mouth
    With a secret

And why, oh, why
    Does it want more
    Than life itself
Swimming free
    On a broken sea"

First Drop

hope swallows hard
on the verge of a cloudburst
where air is so strange and
the sky even stranger in
piled up clouds huddling
holding onto nothing

feel, feel the first drop then
let it sink in
like a stone to the bottom
where nothing's familiar
drifting and tumbling
in slow-motion certainty

I say I can swim
but don't move a limb
just wade a current
gone drifting
to a faraway shore
I dreamt as a child

sifting silent sand into
yellow bucket, red shovel
there's work to be done
on the beach in the sunlight
waves to be waded
and laughter I can still hear

cascading through years
reaching for hope
cast away in surging surf
retrieved vividly
smooth and wet
let it be, just be
until sadness dilutes color

like salt from a tear disappearing
from the day's small fist
covering my eyes
to sleep, to dream and to
hear your voice
one more time

Telescope

There's a telescope staring at the sky tonight
Focusing, yearning for a speck of light
For an endless day in a sea of night
Looking out there to make it all right
    Right here

There are lenses and prisms, and leaded glass
Pulling rainbows and visions and photographs
Exposed through years and the tender past
To the light of the ages' most recent pass
    Right here

But right here, right now
I'm aglow with you
Reflecting on what you've been through

Right here, right now
I'm glowing too
Curving toward the radiance of you

Sunward

Journey to the sun
You'd think would be easy
A straight shot
Following your line of
Sight

The warmth on your face and
Through your clothing
Light
Back along the speed of light

But for the curve of things
    Lazy planets
        On gravity-strings
And impetuous rocks of ice
Collecting speed and color
Halo
Playing off the wall
Behind the net
Slingshot event
    To the black
        Home of stars

Where escape or freedom
    Seems possible
Until years return
    You sunward

Where our foreheads move
        Very close, some
Chakra pull
        Intimate orbit

Your sun-strewn hair
Aurora over my face
Borealis across your
Subtle smile
        And these bodies slowed
In space
Dancing
        As we feel
                Our approach
                      To the Sun
Complete.

Sundown

Sun going down	almost still	moving
sentinel trees stand	feathery filament	testament
touch me	in silhouette	contrast
against new hues	blues	grays

I was bathed	in laughter	lighthearted day
let me drown	in deeper light	heavier light
slipping the hip of	a world turning	from a day
gone	mirthless	heart

    beating darkly across apparent sky
        vanishing
            disappearing arch of azure
                something more
                    fatherless
                        and real

the piercing	point	of first
star	reaching	me
any moment	now	eternal light
lancing	the	eternal night
	of	me

Blacklight

In the blacklight you are indigo
me too, moving limbs weirdly blue
where mine should be – there's you
blue into blue – what glows
reflecting eyes pooling
shadows' liquid light
of you – me – fiercely
facing the source of
joy – liminal lips
invisible in the
dark
grape
taste
of twilight

Rogue

There are planets roaming dark
beyond gone — adrift

lifted from billiard solar systems
galaxy eddies utterly stark
in rapids — soundless

What buildings lay in coal dust ruin
on their frozen surfaces?
What trees beyond petrified
stubble the round faces
of blind planets
homeless?

We are not brought to a final
destination —

Motion, The Journey, is the only
eternity
       and ancient memories
        of a soft moon rising
            long gone

Eclipse

I.

It was only a moon
The moon

And a garden the color of moss
Turned a shade of lichen

Gray and dolorous
Bereft of sun

Holding breath
In the weighty moment

Of the eclipse

II.

That pit in your stomach
Knew the gradual instant

That the full eclipse
Darkened your blood

And left you in the
Pull of the planet

That has desired you
All your life

Against your persistent
Stand for hope

III.

The moon projecting circles
Revealing our gray reality

Colorless, overcast
About to rain

Great terrible moons
Breaking up in the upper atmosphere

Torrential chunks of gray dust
Heavy heaven blanketing

Our eyes
Our great empty hearts

The sinking feeling
Of our sinkhole guts

All neatly filled
With moondust

If I Say I am Afraid

And if I say
I am afraid
You will not know what it is
And vaguely be looking
Beyond me
To that strange light
I never see

But perhaps I am
Casting shadows
Of me

          And of you not seeing me
    Not really

189

I do not see the paper nest
but paper wasps come and go
in awkward dangling flight, swaying and
gracefully alighting on long yellow legs,
antiqued black bodies semi-gloss sheen.

I've never been stung by one,
only by yellow jackets and once a dying
bumble bee I picked up as a child.

I also wear black and yellow stripes
around my conductor's cap
with shiny brim and brass badge
emblazoning my number,
189 —

I am the one hundred eighty-nineth of so
many
like me, as trolleys come and go jangling along
their spiked routes.

Waiting on the hot wooden platform,
occasionally
a paper wasp approaches curious about me
and my fear
      as it hovers considering —
      what to do?

Grasping my brim in one deft arc
I swoop my hat down quickly,
knocking the wasp to the gray planks,
before stomping it hard
it struggles on its back in a papery buzz.

And when the adrenaline subsides
all I can feel is the stomp
on the hollow platform
and what I had crushed
struggling in me
      to live.

Trolley Museum

In the brilliant glow of morning sun
Like a great marble game
Brightly colored streetcars
Roll around sidling
The trolley stop.
Yellow, green, like pines,
Gold paint and yellow lines,
Old numbers faded and reborn
Over cream-white rivets
Throw semi-hemisphere shadows.

All the pretty jelly beans
And hard candies of the
Past two centuries
Still gleam from the
Mouths of the gods of
Time and joy and railway
Dreams.

The ancient art of
Electric poles, inlaid wood,
Coaches, and the
Throb of motors taking points
From the hand of the
Motorman ratcheting the
Controller knob through its arc —

The regular clop and
Clack of rail joints
Shouldering our steel
Wheels cast for the
Journey
To the end of
The line where we
Turn the seats, turn
The pole, and return
The way we came.

A Train Runs Through

A train runs through my life
It clacks and rattles
Sometimes it is heavy
And bends an ancient
Moan from the rail bed

Passengers knit, or sleep

My daughter colors pictures

I can hear the regular
Skitch, skitch, rapid pencil strokes of
     Fields
          Cars
               Trees
Moving in one direction
     Through
          Her life

Orbisonia Dawn

The sun is rising warming walls.
The quiet town groans to life,
Insects yelping, chirping, zinging atop
The heavy sweet meadow grass
Yarrow, burrs, forgotten spices
Waft down the alleys in the
Brightness of the last dreams disjoining.
By an open window we stretch
While the sun is rising
On cotton sheets.
I stand by the gentle curtain warming my
Adobe skin.

Rockhill Furnace had coke oven heart
Overgrown, crumbling like Christ-tombs
Gaping hidden
On the edge of town,
Across the tracks,
Blacklog Creek runs clear and thin rippling
Into the morning.

A killdeer spirits over the pebbled
Parking lot.
A church bell pierces startled air
And air things hawking, inhaling it know the
Soaring peal came from the black iron thing
Long ago rolled away, cindered breath
Dissipated up to heaven, long ago.

Steam engine spirits haunt this town
Retiring in mountain mines given up
Their golden bells to churches,
Golden hearts removed, transplanted,
Calling the mothers, fathers, children
To take a seat and ride
The last trip to the skies,
To the mines, to the hope of our
Thin-walled fragile hearts
When coke ovens stand cold.

Altered State

The day you drove the
Steam engine through the
Back wall of the engine house
On Central Street
And precariously up the grassy hill
Toward Freddie Greens's barn
Without the aid of track —
Bricks popping out of place
Rear wall exploding
Where you plowed
A magnificent hole

The engine house did not fall.
The other engine — the "Watatic"
Was unperturbed.
Neighbors wanted their
Pictures taken next to the
Spectacle of the wreck.
Everyone under the sun came out
To gawk and talk and consider
The weight of these things —
How to move them —
Get back on track.

It was the first day of
Your sobriety and
Your last day on
The Ashburnham Railroad

But the railroad's gone now
The engine house disappeared over years
Like coal smoke and cinders
To the sky —
    And you —

    You're still sober.

Daring Duo

Coyotes and bobcats have been spotted
in my rural New England town. Not actually spotted, but
there have been sightings. And not together, never
together, having the same approximate jobs.
Like competing dentists, we are obliged to see
one or the other as they extract what they must.

It was a very good year for chipmunks and they
knew it, leaping to and fro through low garden fences
in rapid succession like long furry ping pong balls
in a heated match. And so much like flying Mars bars
that
it became a very good year for coyotes
and bobcats as well — but never together.

Which makes me imagine, if coyotes and bobcats
were to join forces what wonders they could accomplish.
Perhaps they do when we are not looking,
and pursue bigger game after polishing off
tapirs, emus, coatis — I haven't seen a single tapir
in the four years I've lived here.

They might be protecting us, the coyote and
the bobcat, like superheroes teaming up to
defeat an alien menace. Muscular in their gray fur
outfits. Come to think of it,
no one has spotted a Bengal tiger or a Kodiak bear in
all of Worcester county this year. Not one.

Let us give thanks to the coyotes and bobcats,
for putting aside their differences, and
teaming up just this once for all time, while we,
in our homes, avoiding deadly viruses, breathe easy,
and watch from our windows, cell phones poised,
ready to capture one final heroic escapade:
coyote and bobcat,
united to save the world.

Prodigal

I think of Pennsylvania on days like this.
The arching sunsets over a bowl horizon,
the curvy fields' lumpy land undulating
years back to me crashing Appalachian
surf of time rolled up with ancestors
neatly filed below marked weathered stone.
Only I am missing.

I return, having lost some
things from my rucksack,
an accent heavy and round as potatoes
drumming down a wooden chute in a barn,
an unrequited love who never wrote back
or returned my calls, all my life.
The candle I held for him.

Places like home, or a house, or a
bedroom, or just an old gray-green wooden bed
that had been my great grandmother Chee's.

Grandparents, great grandparents, laughter
twinkling eyes or stars in the night song
of a child voice.
Prayers piercing the dark.

I was loved. I do keep that
close, so close I hope it can breathe.
My arms are much stronger now.
Longer.
And there's so much less to hold
tightly.

I Was a Psychologist

I was a psychologist in the year of plague
    when we kept our selves to ourselves
and the police state baffled every cop
    we knew as friend —
as media fed our heads afraid

So there was a lot for a therapist to do
    with seeping hearts calling
expanding in small rooms —
    a studio grew in my guestroom
the way wasps build nests and one day
    there's this buzzing papery machine

with a good camera and two-in-one-laptop
    and indirect lighting
I sat in my Victorian room
    broadcasting HIPPA-compliant hope
to each soul trapped
    in the oddly calm days of loss

and kept the trauma manuals
    within easy reach —
just out of sight on the guestroom bed
    quilted by a grandmother gone —
and spoke of gone-ness
    and what's beyond

And after a neighbor mowed his lawn
        his apoplectic dog had its hour
to vent a limbic scream at anyone who moved
        a limb — but we all scream —
as stormtroopers arrive in heavy gear
        shooting canisters of gas to clear a path

And even in the updated version with better CGI
        Darth Vader still stumbles
striding over the bodies of the rebellion

I close my two-paned window
        as the Deathstar gyrates
to life — or death
        and my house is the first
on my street
        to burst to flames

What to do with the Body —

I mean my body — after it is no longer
my body.
I had some vague notion of a grave,
a lot of silence, fairly consistently cool,
and worms frustrated by 21st century technology —
a well-sealed sarcophagus and casket —
the squelching of things circling and swimming around
like wormy sharks, unable to get in,
and vaguely swearing under their worm-breath,

when, this morning, after performing the Abbots
Bromley, an ancient ritual dance,
dressed as a deer — in a way
only ancient people would have found deer-ish —
while de-antlering and removing our leafy masks
and scarlet hoods, Al and Kirk were talking about
cannons and how there's this guy in New Hampshire
who will shoot your ashes from a brass cannon
with a deafening explosion. Listening — I became
transfixed.

That mixture of ash-me with black powder
ignited and forced with flame and fury
through a small brass bore
in the live-free-or-die state is perfect!
To go out with a bang,
after whatever brought me to ash has passed.
It's the dance, the ritual, the last leap,
the blasted love of life grinning like smoke wide
white and sliding sideways across a blue sky —
my final spiritual escapade played out
the way smoke from a cannon flies and fades.

I feel a tingling sense of peace and excitement
like the "ooh" and "ahh" on the fourth of July,
knowing no matter what I do today,
quietly or half-hearted, in love or jest,
it's all enough. It's okay. Because
it all ends with my body moving other bodies,
resounding, dancing against the pounding chests of
anyone within earshot. One last Yippee!
Teeth, dust, bones, crowns, split ears
and all in a great cloud of thundering ash.
Who knew the hills could rock in my wake as
I go out with a blast?

Seed

My life is male but not masculine — often
as not-my-life is woman — but not woman

This — none of it identifies who I am —
that is no mystery

The turning fuchsia hang from
my porch in autumn noon light

bright yellow leaves are there — were not
yesterday

and I watch them from the music room's
plush floral sofa

because I am cold — my fingers
even as I write this — seek warmth

in words from a crystal pen
curiously free from ideas engendered

There is simply me and — next
like dancing fuchsia

in my half-spin — the label
peeled from the pot long ago

when I was a seed suspended in
        black soil

What To Do

The wicker rocking chair
The company of companion poems
The remaining birdsongs this afternoon —
    What has this to do with me?

The slate roof — color of the street below
The leaves fallen from the plant in blue glaze
To the floorboards' old sheen —
    What have they to do with me?

The guest room window curtain's caress
The quilted bed besot with books
Framed girl in garden green gazing on —
    What have you to do with me?

The desire to read or nap easily
The lonely hour of dream or love recalled
The pen pressed here to this tiny page —
    What have I to do
        with me?

Returning Home by Pleasant Street

"Well, they are gone, and here I must remain"
    — Samuel Taylor Coleridge

    Well, it's summer
    Well, it's morning
    Well it is by the ogive window
    of our cottage
    the haze-thick sky
    shrouds my shoulders, neck, eyes
    searching it through for hints of blue
    to come

    in humid languor I relent
    Lover, you have me at my ease
    though they pave
    Pleasant Street
    and the birds chirrup and call
    for all their small-throated hearts

    A distant piano repeats pensive refrains
    again again Schumann
    being learned in the heart and fingers
    of the soul I know best —
    the one who lives the other half
    of this romantic cottagery —

    I loved you from the first
    hot summer before the pinewood
    glade, and love carried us
    to this dreamy day
    a block from Pleasant Street
    in its heat, repaved

the calm air cooled pretends a breeze
morning light defines some
color in a brighter mood
even the haze lets down its
guard to a fathomless deep
eternity over our street

We might stroll together hand in hand
as we often do
to Chapel Street, Meetinghouse Hill

and down along the Free Meadow Fields
to the Central Way

Yet our laughter and animated talk
flashes best for me as we
return home
       by Pleasant Street

Notes

"189" was in fact the number assigned to me by the Shade Gap Electric Railway in the 1970s, now the Rockhill Trolley Museum.

"Altered State" takes liberty with history. There was such an accident, however, the "Watatic" engine was no longer in service at that time, and the railroad had become a branch of the Boston and Maine, rather than the Ashburnham Railroad.

"Arroyo" is a river that comes and goes, at times raging, at other times dry.

"Autumn Will" is a form I call a Fold Poem. It unfolds its initial stanza both physically and conceptually and aims for symmetry in various ways before folding itself again along the way it came.

"Corner Seat in an Ashburnham Gallery" was inspired by the digital photo on canvas, *Meeting House,* by Joe Cantor, and makes reference to the Creative Connections art galleries in Ashburnham, MA, where there had previously been a prayer center.

"Dandelion Fairy." Alaya has many meanings across cultures and stories since its Sanskrit origins, most of which apply here.

"Help! I Need Some Body" was inspired by the sculpture, *Help,* by Michael Greenburg, with a nod to The Beatles.

"i and you" was written after E. E. Cummings.

"In Reply," besides echoing the Beatles, repeats the first three words of Jesus in the Bible.

"Maple Wings" was inspired by the sculpture *Consume* by Todd Bartel.

"New Vision" was inspired by Patti Smith.

"Open Sway" was inspired by the sculpture *Pods Aloft* by Trish Dehls.

"Orbisonia Dawn" makes reference to a steam engine's bell becoming a church bell in town, which is true.

"Slow Silver." The petite daisies here, when daisies are no more, are actually wood asters.

"Stasis" was inspired by the sculpture *Frozen in Life* by Anna Thurber.

"Teine Sith" contains references to Will-O-the-Wisp mythologies from various countries.

"The Mushroom Garden" was inspired by the sculpture *My Garden* by Cecelia Lamancusa.

"This Time Around" was inspired by the sculpture *Full Circle* by Bob Kephart.

"Uncoiling" was inspired by the sculptures *Continuous Line I* & *Continuous Line II* by Kelly Goff, and is dedicated in loving memory to Steve Schwartz.

"Voice Above the Waves" owes a debt to James Martin's book, *Jesus: A Pilgrimage,* for giving me the concept of Jesus using water as a sound system.

"Waiting to Rain" makes references to George Harrison's song, "So Sad," and Mikhail Lermontov's novel, *A Hero of Our Time.*

"What To Do" owes inspiration, in part, to the painting, *In the Hawthorn Hedge* by Carl Larsson.

"What to do With the Body —" Al and Kirk, of the poem, have since corrected me. The cannon is iron, not brass. Abbotts Bromley has ancient origins lost in the mists of time, but likely as far back as when people first began wearing animal bits to celebrate both people and animals and the circle of life.

Acknowledgments

Grateful acknowledgment is made to the editors of the following publications in which these poems, or earlier versions of them were accepted for publication:

Amethyst Review: "The Way"

Anti-Heroin Chic: "Going On"

Asylum Magazine: "Seed"

Attachment: New Directions in Psychotherapy and Relational Analysis: "If I Say I Am Afraid"

Black Moon Magazine: "189"

Cacti Fur: "Daring Duo"

The Chelmsford Poetry Review: "Kerouac Rain," "Orbisonia Dawn"

Door is A Jar Magazine: "Ajar," "The Paper Door"

Entropy Magazine: "Need Not"

Feelings of the Heart: "Emptying Clouds," "My Heart Ensnared"

Fiddles and Scribbles: "Blacklight"

Friends Journal: "A Kinder Solitude"

Global Poemic: "I Was a Psychologist"

Golden Walkman Magazine: "The Cart Path"

Harpy Hybrid Review: "Prodigal," "Sundown"

Heavy Feather Review: "Chill November," "Closest Thing," "Crossing the Dark Wing," "Presence"

Highveld Poetry Review: "A Train Runs Through," "Trolley Museum"

Insulatus: "Rogue," "What to Do"

Litterateur: "In Reply"

Manuscript: "New Season"

Monadnock Underground: "The Sea, The Sea," "Voice Above the Waves," "What to do with the Body—"

Musings: "Against Gray," "All You Need Bring," "Falling Song," "Fatigues," "New England Dulcimer," "Not Me," "On the Steps," "On the Surface," "Shadow Fences," "The String," "Waiting to Rain"

Otherwise Engaged Literature and Arts Journal: "Gray Hullaballoo," "i and you," "New Vision"

Pif Magazine: "Atmosphere"

POETiCA REViEW: "Disassembled"

Sylvia Magazine: "Autumn Will"

Until the Stars Burn Out: "Eclipse," "Sunward," "Telescope"

Wild Musette Journal: "Dance"

The following poems appeared in anthologies and the editors are gratefully acknowledged: "Open Sway," "Stasis," "This Time Around" in *Art on the Trails: Exposure* (Route 7 Press); "Help! I Need Some Body," "The Mushroom Garden," "Uncoiling" in *Art on the Trails: Rising Up* (Route 7 Press); "Arroyo," "First Drop," and "Untitled" (appearing with the title "Ice Flow") in *Cascades and Currents* (Quabbin Quills); "Altered State," "Returning Home by Pleasant Street" in *From the Soil: A Hometown Anthology* (Exeter Publishing); "A Day in June," "Seeing" in *In a Field of Dandelions* (Maya McCormick Press); "Dandelion Fairy," "Maple Wings," "Slow Silver," "Teine Sith," "Walk With Me" in *Into the Glen: Into the Light* (Fae Corps Inc Publishing); "Attic Haunt" in *Psythur* (Ravens Quoth Press).

"Darkening Trees" was a 2023 winner of Poetry in the Pines from the Monadnock Writers' Group. It is installed on the Grassy Pond Trail at the Cathedral in the Pines in Rindge, New Hampshire.

"Corner Seat in an Ashburnham Gallery" appeared in the gallery at *Creative Connections* in Ashburnham, Massachusetts.

"A Kinder Solitude," "Closest Thing," "Presence," and "Prodigal" were featured on *Bespoke Vocals by Kirk Lawrence* on YouTube at www.youtube.com/user/itskirklawrence

Gratitude

For Carl Mabbs-Zeno at Khotso Publishing for suggesting this project and for expertly seeing it through to this fine volume that you now hold in your hands.

For 'Rena Gerhard, the first poet I ever knew, my mother, who led me to read great poets and great literature and was delighted to encourage me as a poet all my life.

For my father, J. Calvin Gerhard, the most steadfast man I know and a constant support.

For Steven Schwartz, my brother in writing, in music, and in Christ. My first true poet friend. He would have loved this.

For Ann Louise Wanner, the first teacher to truly inspire me to write and to believe that I could. A great mentor.

For my teachers in the English departments at Wilkes College and Kutztown University, especially Harry Humes, for his course in writing poetry where I really first thought seriously about how to hone my writing.

For Mary-Ellen Gerhard and Florence Johnson, my grandmothers, the former a constant promoter of anything I wrote who proudly shared my work. And the latter, a poet, and a loving soul who I wish could have seen this.

For Ed Wilfert, my honorary uncle and lifelong mentor and friend. He always encouraged me to read and live outside of the box, and to really explore words in a playful way.

For Jack Gerhard, my brother and friend, and the only person to actually ask for and put my words to music.

For Gregg Januszewski, my best friend and comrade, endlessly supportive, and goofy, and wise.

For Cecilia Januszewski, consummate writer, who always steered me toward great writers and literary ideas. She also was the first person to challenge me to write daily, a process that continues to this day.

For Sophia Januszewski who did the artwork for the cover. She's also a fine poet.

For Barbara Morrison whose retreats gave me the courage to workshop poems and to really see myself as a poet in the company of other writers.

For Kirk Lawrence-Howard who took up the mantle of daily poetry performances during the onset of the pandemic. He's been ceaselessly supportive and encouraging of my poetry. He's also a fine poet.

For anyone who, knowing or unknowing, was ever a friend to me in writing. You are not forgotten. Blessed be.

For new friends in literary groups: Quabbin Quills, The Worcester County Poetry Association, especially my newfound brother, the poet Robert Eugene Perry, The Monadnock Writers' Group, where I met Carl Mabbs-Zeno, and the New Dawn Writers' Group, especially Kevin, Abby, Melissa, Simon, Pat, Heidi, and the whole crew who comes out to write or read. I am grateful.

For friends with whom I've danced: Pinewoods, The Jacks, and the contra community. Your impact is evident through most of this work.

For ancestors, whose work sparked something in me to keep writing, especially Jacob R. Totheroh and Paul Gerhardt.

For my children, whom I love more than I can express. I know. I've tried. For their suggestions of books and ideas, and their encouragement. And for my family near and far. Yes, you.

And especially, and most of all, for Rachael, the love of my life, my sometime reader and editor, her humor, talent, wit, music, and honesty. I love you. You are my favorite human being.

About the Author

Fred Gerhard's poems have appeared in numerous magazines and anthologies including *Entropy Magazine, Friends Journal, Harpy Hybrid Review, Heavy Feather Review, Monadnock Underground, Pif Magazine, POETiCA REViEW,* and *Sylvia Magazine*. His ekphrastic poetry has been on exhibit in the Creative Connections art gallery in Ashburnham, Massachusetts. His poetry has also been voiced by actor Kirk Lawrence on Bespoke Vocals, as seen on YouTube. He is one of the 2023 winners of the Poetry in the Pines contest for which his work is installed on the trails at the Cathedral in the Pines in Rindge, New Hampshire.

He was the editor for the *Chelmsford Poetry Review,* and is currently an editor for Quabbin Quills press anthologies, and for *Smoky Quartz - An Online Journal of Literature & Art.*

Fred Gerhard is one of the founders of the New Dawn Writers' Group in Ashburnham where he leads monthly poetry workshops, and helps host open mic nights. For many years he ran a poetry therapy group at Community Healthlink in Worcester, MA. He currently runs a Facebook group to help bring together and support local poets and authors. He is a member of the Worcester County Poetry Association, the Monadnock Writers' Group, and the New England Poetry Club, and thrives on taking part in readings and getting to know other poets.

www.ingramcontent.com/pod-product-compliance
Lightning Source LLC
Chambersburg PA
CBHW030001110526
44587CB00011BA/1060